BRINGING BACK THE
Whooping Crane

Rachel Stuckey

CRABTREE
PUBLISHING COMPANY
WWW.CRABTREEBOOKS.COM

CRABTREE
PUBLISHING COMPANY
WWW.CRABTREEBOOKS.COM

Author: Rachel Stuckey

Series Research and Development: Reagan Miller

Managing Editor: Tim Cooke

Picture Manager: Sophie Mortimer

Design Manager: Keith Davis

Editorial Director: Lindsey Lowe

Children's Publisher: Anne O'Daly

Editor: Ellen Rodger

Proofreader: Lorna Notsch

Cover design: Margaret Amy Salter

**Production coordinator and
   Prepress technician:** Margaret Amy Salter

Print coordinator: Katherine Berti

Produced for Crabtree Publishing Company
by Brown Bear Books

Photographs (t=top, b= bottom, l=left, r=right, c=center)

Front Cover: All images from Shutterstock

Interior: Alamy: Mark J. Barrett, 9b, Danita Delimont, 16, LDWF, 14,
PureStock, 20; Courtesy of the Allen Family, 13; AP: Tom Sistack, 15b;
Aurora Photos: Tom Lynn, 15t; Dreamstime: Norman Bateman, 5, Lynn
Bystrom, 10, Jeffrey Holcombe, 19t; Getty Images: Wild Horizon/UIG, 18;
International Crane Foundation: 17; iStock: Bob Canon, 7, franksvlli, 26,
Kellington1, 1, Michael Roeder, 11; Public Domain: Quadell, 25;
Shutterstock: Connie Barr, 4, Ivan C, 29, Tony Campbell, 19b, critterbiz,
9t, Nicole S Glass, 28; Stephen L. Tabone Photography: 27t, 27b; Texas
Public Radio: David Martin Davies, 22; Whooping Crane Association of
North America: Silva Leanne, 24.

Brown Bear Books has made every attempt to contact the copyright
holder. If you have any information please contact licensing@
brownbearbooks.co.uk

Library and Archives Canada Cataloguing in Publication

Stuckey, Rachel, author
      Bringing back the whooping crane / Rachel Stuckey.

(Animals back from the brink)
Includes index.
Issued in print and electronic formats.
ISBN 978-0-7787-4906-6 (hardcover).--
ISBN 978-0-7787-4939-4 (softcover).--
ISBN 978-1-4271-2106-6 (HTML)

      1. Whooping crane--Juvenile literature. 2. Whooping crane--
Conservation--Juvenile literature. 3. Endangered species--Juvenile
literature. 4. Wildlife recovery--Juvenile literature. I. Title.

QL696.G84S77 2018   j333.95'832   C2018-903055-0
                                                C2018-903056-9

Library of Congress Cataloging-in-Publication Data

Names: Stuckey, Rachel, author.
Title: Bringing back the whooping crane / Rachel Stuckey.
Description: New York, New York : Crabtree Publishing, [2019] |
   Series: Animals back from the brink | Includes index.
Identifiers: LCCN 2018036871 (print) | LCCN 2018037483 (ebook) |
   ISBN 9781427121066 (Electronic) |
   ISBN 9780778749066 (hardcover : alk. paper) |
   ISBN 9780778749394 (paperback : alk. paper)
Subjects: LCSH: Whooping crane--North America--Conservation--
   Juvenile literature.
Classification: LCC QL696.G84 (ebook) |
   LCC QL696.G84 S789 2019 (print) | DDC 598.3/2--dc23
LC record available at https://lccn.loc.gov/2018036871

Crabtree Publishing Company
www.crabtreebooks.com   1-800-387-7650

Printed in the U.S.A./102018/CG20180810

**Published in Canada
Crabtree Publishing**
616 Welland Ave.
St. Catharines, Ontario
L2M 5V6

**Published in the United States
Crabtree Publishing**
PMB 59051
350 Fifth Avenue, 59th Floor
New York, New York 10118

**Published in the United Kingdom
Crabtree Publishing**
Maritime House
Basin Road North, Hove
BN41 1WR

**Published in Australia
Crabtree Publishing**
3 Charles Street
Coburg North
VIC, 3058

Contents

Find videos and extra material online at **crabtreeplus.com** to learn more about the conservation of animals and ecosystems. See page 30 in this book for the access code to this material.

Larger Than Life

The whooping crane is a remarkable sight—but few people ever see it because it is one of the rarest birds in North America. In the 1900s, the crane almost became extinct due to loss of **habitat**. The bird is named for its loud call, which can be heard from miles (kilometers) away. The whooping crane was once common. The birds spent the summer in the northern United States and Canada. They flew south for the winter to the **wetlands** around the Gulf of Mexico, stopping in other wetlands along the way.

The whooping crane is the tallest bird in North America, at almost 5 feet (1.5 m). It has a wingspan of 7.5 feet (2.3 m). When it spreads its wings to fly, the whooping crane is as big as a professional basketball player.

Whooping cranes are o
species of cranes in No
The adults have bright
feathers with black ti
black bill, and a red cr
crown is the top of th

BY THE NUMBERS

The whooping crane has always been relatively rare. Scientists estimate that before Europeans arrived, there were just over 10,000 whooping cranes in North America. In comparison, there are five million Canada geese, 13 million blue jays, and 120 million cardinals in North America today. During the expansion of U.S. settlement in the 1800s, hunting and habitat destruction reduced the number of whooping cranes to just 1,400 by 1870. In the early 1940s, the species was almost **extinct**. Scientists counted just 21 whooping cranes in the wild, plus two birds living in **captivity**. Today, conservation efforts have meant the whooping crane has come back from the brink. Of a total of almost 600 birds, about 435 are in the wild and 165 in captivity.

Species at Risk

Created in 1984, the International Union for the **Conservation** of Nature (IUCN) protects wildlife, plants, and **natural resources** around the world. Its members include about 1,400 governments and nongovernmental organizations. The IUCN publishes the Red List of Threatened **Species** each year, which tells people how likely a plant or animal species is to become extinct. It began publishing the list in 1964.

SCIENTIFIC CRITERIA

The Red List, created by scientists, divides nearly 80,000 species of plants and animals into nine categories. Criteria for each category include the growth and **decline** of the population size of a species. They also include how many individuals within a species can breed, or have babies. In addition scientists include information about the habitat of the species, such as its size and quality. These criteria allow scientists to figure out the probability of extinction facing the species.

Darwin's fox lives in Chilé. In 2004 and 2008, the Red List classified it as Critically Endangered (CR), but in 2016, its status was changed to Endangered (EN). The IUCN Red List is updated twice a year to track the changing of species. Each individual species is reevaluated at least every five years.

IUCN LEVELS OF THREAT

The Red List uses nine categories to define the threat to a species.

Extinct (EX)	No living individuals survive
Extinct in the Wild (EW)	Species cannot be found in its natural habitat. Exists only in captivity, in **cultivation**, or in an area that is not its natural habitat.
Critically Endangered (CR)	At extremely high risk of becoming extinct in the wild
Endangered (EN)	At very high risk of extinction in the wild
Vulnerable (VU)	At high risk of extinction in the wild
Near Threatened (NT)	Likely to become threatened in the near future
Least Concern (LC)	Widespread, abundant, or at low risk
Data Deficient (DD)	Not enough data to make a judgment about the species
Not Evaluated (NE)	Not yet evaluated against the criteria

In the United States, the Endangered Species Act of 1973 was passed to protect species from possible extinction. It has its own criteria for classifying species, but they are similar to those of the IUCN. Canada introduced the Species at Risk Act in 2002. More than 530 species are protected under the act. The list of species is compiled by the Committee on the Status of Endangered Wildlife in Canada (COSEWIC).

WHOOPING CRANES AT RISK

The IUCN Red List has classified the whooping crane as Endangered since 1994. In 2016, the list noted that the population was increasing. Since 1967, the bird has also been listed as Endangered by the Endangered Species Act in the United States.

Shrinking Habitat

Whooping cranes once ranged over the midwestern United States and Canada. In the late 1800s, increased human settlement disturbed the wilderness. Towns and cities grew, and much of the cranes' habitat disappeared. In the past, cranes wintered around the coast of the Gulf of Mexico. Today, they are limited to one site at Aransas, Texas. A single hurricane could destroy this winter site and threaten the birds' survival. The National Audubon Society is a conservation group founded in 1905 to protect birds in North America. It predicts that, by 2080, the whooping crane may lose another 85 percent of its winter habitat because of **climate change**.

Whooping crane habitat has been threatened for centuries as settlers drained wetlands and plowed prairies to create farmland. The settlers also hunted cranes and took their eggs for food. Within a few centuries, the already small population declined to just 1,400 birds.

COLLABORATING FOR A CAUSE

When the population of whooping cranes reached its lowest point in the 1940s, people living along the birds' migration route saw fewer birds each year. In the 1950s, concerned individuals formed the Whooper Club. They started to write to government officials about the disappearing crane. In 1961, the Whooper Club became the Whooping Crane Conservation Association (WCCA). The WCCA also included U.S. and Canadian scientists. This group began raising awareness not just with the government, but also with the public. In 1967, the whooping crane was listed as threatened with extinction.

The main **flock** of whooping cranes **migrates** south along the central flyway. The cranes breed in the swampy bogs of the Wood Buffalo National Park in northern Alberta but winter in the wetlands of the Aransas National Wildlife Refuge in Texas.

Ecosystem Threats

...g cranes are not just
...e because of their
... habitat. In the past,
...unted whooping cranes
...meat and feathers,
...cted their eggs. Today,
...face threats from
...s such as ravens,
...olves, black bears,
...Many adult whooping
...re still killed by
...s, such as bobcats in
...One of the most
...causes of premature
...when these huge birds
...ower lines. Even the
...g cranes that live in
...face threats. In 2007,
...e whooping cranes
...ed in a lightning strike.
...h of any breeding
...g crane is a threat to
...e population.

Whooping cranes usually lay just one or two eggs. Once the egg hatches, the chick faces many dangers from predators or from being orphaned if its parents are killed by predators or by other causes.

A DOMINO EFFECT

An **ecosystem** works like a line of falling dominos—one change leads to another. In Florida, the Florida panther was a top predator that fed on bobcats (right). When the panther population fell, bobcats flourished. More bobcats needed more food, so they hunted more whooping cranes. On the Gulf Coast, whooping cranes eat blue crab and wolfberries. In 2009, a **drought** reduced the population of blue crab, and fewer wolfberries grew. This small change had a major effect. Twice the number of cranes died that year than did the year before.

WHOOPING CRANE HISTORICAL RANGE

CANADA

UNITED STATES

MEXICO

The whooping crane's breeding **range** used to stretch over much of the midwestern United States. The birds migrated south to spend the winter in various locations, mainly along the coast of the Gulf of Mexico. In the past, the coastal wetlands had many crabs, other amphibians, fish, and wolfberries, but these food supplies have fallen.

Key
Historical range

■ Breeding (summer) range

■ Wintering range

0   620 miles
├──────────┤
      1,000 km

Who Got Involved?

From the start, saving the whooping crane was a team effort among scientists and researchers, government agencies, bird enthusiasts, and citizens in both Canada and the United States. Conservation efforts were also a collaboration between government agencies and other organizations. The early efforts were started by the National Audubon Society, one of the oldest conservation organizations in the United States. It joined with the U.S. Fish and Wildlife Service to protect the whooping crane in 1945. In the 1950s, the Whooper Club brought together scientists and bird lovers to urge governments in Canada and the United States to protect the cranes. Today, efforts to save the whooping crane are managed by the International Whooping Crane Recovery Team, which includes scientists and conservation officials from both Canada and the United States.

The International Crane Foundation (ICF) leads global efforts to protect all species of cranes. It was founded in 1973 by U.S. **ornithologist** George W. Archibald and his colleagues.

BOOST FROM A GAME SHOW

One of the first whooping crane heroes was Robert Porter Allen (left), an ornithologist with the National Audubon Society. In 1962, Dr. Allen appeared on a game show called *To Tell the Truth*. On the show, a celebrity panel had to ask three men claiming to be Dr. Allen about whooping cranes. It was a very popular game show, and Dr. Allen's appearance helped to raise public awareness about the shrinking population of the endangered birds.

COLLABORATING FOR A CAUSE

The effort to save the whooping crane relies on many organizations working together. For example, the Whooping Crane Eastern Partnership (WCEP) has worked to create a new migrating flock of cranes in the eastern United States. The WCEP has more than 10 different partners:

- International Whooping Crane Recovery Team
- International Crane Foundation (ICF)
- Operation Migration (OM)
- Patuxent Wildlife Research Center
- National Fish and Wildlife Foundation
- USGS National Wildlife Health Center
- U.S. Fish and Wildlife Service (USFWS)
- U.S. Geological Survey (USGS)
- Wisconsin Department of Natural Resources (WDNR)
- Natural Resources Foundation of Wisconsin (NRF).
- Florida Fish and Wildlife Conservation Commission (FFWCC)

Getting a Team Together

After the whooping crane was named an Endangered species, the United States and Canada both began working to save the crane. In 1995, they combined their efforts to create the International Whooping Crane Recovery Team. The team has five members from the United States and five from Canada. These experts in birds and conservation meet each year and invite other experts to help them plan future conservation efforts. Then government agencies of both countries must approve the plans. The Whooping Crane Recovery Team wants the whooping crane to be reclassified from Endangered to Threatened.

A captive population of whooping cranes is kept in pens at the White Lake Wetlands Conservation Area in Louisiana. The birds were reintroduced to the state in 2011. By 2014, the wild flock numbered 40 birds. The first two eggs hatched in Louisiana in 2016.

INTERNATIONAL RECOVERY PLAN

The International Recovery Team published the first International Recovery Plan for the whooping crane in 1986. The plan's purpose was to coordinate research and conservation efforts in the United States and Canada to eventually remove the whooping crane from the Endangered Species List. The plan aimed to protect the wild population and its habitat. It also aimed to increase the population of captive birds, so that new populations could be introduced into the wild. To be sure of survival, the whooping crane needs to have multiple wild flocks. Some flocks are migrating, such as the population that migrates from Wood Buffalo National Park in Alberta, Canada to Aransas National Wildlife Refuge in Texas. Others are nonmigrating, such as the whooping cranes in Louisiana.

Each flock must breed successfully to maintain its own population, and each flock must be large enough to survive a disaster, such as a hurricane or a drought. Many efforts are underway to help wild whooping cranes increase their population.

One initiative adopted by the Crane Recovery Team has been to teach captive-bred whooping cranes to migrate by encouraging them to follow a pilot in an **ultra-lightweight aircraft**.

Going into Action

Whooping cranes live between 22 and 24 years, but they face many threats in the wild, and many die early. Only a few wild mating pairs have young each year. Each pair has only one or two eggs a year, and only one chick usually lives to adulthood. Such a low birth rate makes it difficult for the population to grow. The earliest efforts to save whooping cranes involved helping them to breed. Scientists began by using **artificial insemination** to fertilize crane eggs. The real challenge came in teaching the chicks how to behave as adults without having the example of parents to follow.

Adult whooping cranes teach their young what to eat. Whooping cranes mainly eat shellfish, small fish, insects, amphibians such as frogs, and reptiles. However, they have a wide diet and also eat grains, acorns, and plants that live in the wetlands they visit.

A TRIAL WITH FOSTER PARENTS

An early attempt to save the whooping crane involved the sandhill crane, North America's other crane species. In 1975, scientists put fertilized whooping crane eggs in sandhill nests in Idaho. The sandhill cranes hatched 85 eggs. The whooping cranes were fostered by the sandhills and learned to migrate to the Rio Grande in Mexico. However, when the whooping cranes reached breeding age, they tried to mate with sandhill cranes and failed to breed. The project ended in 1989. Today, no whooping cranes live with Idaho sandhill cranes.

COLLABORATING FOR A CAUSE

In the 1970s, 10 of the world's 15 crane species were endangered. George W. Archibald, a young Canadian ornithologist, wanted to change that. He cofounded the International Crane Foundation in the United States in 1973, and served as its director until 2000. Archibald helped to develop methods for breeding and raising cranes in captivity. In 1976, he lived with a female whooping crane named Tex (below right). Tex's eggs were artificially inseminated, and one crane chick was hatched. Named Gee Wiz, the young male crane survived and eventually mated with a female crane. Archibald has spent his life saving the whooping crane, winning many awards for his efforts.

Challenging Tasks

The Whooping Crane Recovery Team focuses on captive breeding and reintroduction. However, there are threats the team cannot defend against, such as climate change and pollution that damage the cranes' habitat. Global warming is causing sea levels to rise. This is changing the Texas wetlands where the migrating flock spends the winter. As salt water floods the wetlands, the water and food supply change. Climate change is also causing more droughts, which affect the breeding grounds in the north, the wetlands along the migration routes, and the winter nesting grounds.

George Archibald developed **costume method** for humans to raise whooping cranes. Human handlers dress in crane costumes in order to teach young birds to act like adult whooping cranes. In an alternate method called parent rearing, captive adult cranes raise the chicks.

A SETBACK FOR THE PROGRAM

In 1993, the Whooping Crane Recovery Team began a program to build a nonmigrating flock in Kissimmee in Florida (below). Nonmigrating birds spend the entire year in their nesting grounds. These birds were hatched and raised in captivity. Over the following decade, 289 captive-bred birds were introduced into the habitat. However, the population did not thrive. Bobcats and alligators ate the birds, and drought caused habitat loss. By 2006, only 53 birds survived. The recovery team decided not to introduce any more birds unless survival rates improved. In 2015, there were fewer than 10 cranes left in Kissimmee. In 2018, the U.S. Fish and Wildlife service proposed moving these birds to join the nonmigrating crane flock in Louisiana.

The wild whooping cranes' migration route is called the central **flyway**. Historically, it allowed the cranes to find wetlands easily. Today, droughts caused by climate change sometimes mean these key wetlands are completely dry.

Making Some Progress

The only remaining wild flock of migrating whooping cranes is the Aransas–Wood Buffalo population. These birds migrate through the prairies of Canada and the midwestern United States from northern Alberta to coastal Texas. However, the Whooping Crane Eastern Partnership has reintroduced a new flock of migrating cranes into the eastern United States.

This new flock was hatched and raised in captivity at the Patuxent Wildlife Research Center in Maryland, then moved to the Necedah National Wildlife Refuge in Wisconsin. The population began in 2001, when 10 whooping cranes were transported to Wisconsin. That year, eight birds migrated down the eastern flyway to Florida. Eventually, the flock grew as new birds were introduced.

Captive-bred birds do not migrate south on their own. They must be taught to fly south. The population in Wisconsin was taught to migrate using aircraft-led migration. The technique was first developed by a pilot who trained orphaned Canada geese to migrate south in the 1980s.

COLLABORATING FOR A CAUSE

Operation Migration is an organization that helps reintroduce migrating birds into the wild by teaching them to migrate. Operation Migration pilots use ultra-light aircraft to fly at the head of the flock and lead birds to winter nesting grounds. The process takes weeks, as the birds must stop along the way to rest. Before they can migrate, the birds must **imprint** on the aircraft. Newly hatched chicks will trust and follow the first thing they see after they hatch. The crane chicks learn to follow the aircraft in a special pen. As they mature, they go on daily practice flights to get them ready for their fall migration. Then the pilot leads the cranes from Wisconsin along a safe migration route to nesting grounds in Florida.

When cranes do not have parents, human handlers teach them to imprint on the aircraft by wearing costumes and using puppets. They also run aircraft engines close to the chicks or use recordings of the aircraft to get the chicks used to the sound.

Success Story in Louisiana

Beginning in 2011, scientists began an effort to create a new nonmigrating population of whooping cranes in Louisiana. Scientists released 10 to 16 juveniles each year into the White Lake Wetlands Conservation Area or the Rockefeller Wildlife Refuge. The goal of the project is to have 25 breeding pairs. In 2016, five pairs of cranes mated, and the first whooping crane in the flock was successfully hatched. By 2018, there were almost 60 birds in the flock. The struggling nonmigrating population in Florida may be moved to join this Louisiana flock.

During the crane migration, around 80,000 people visit Nebraska to watch the Aransas–Wood Buffalo birds on their way back to Canada. In winter, Port Aransas, Texas, holds an annual festival to celebrate the cranes. Visitors spend millions of dollars on hotels and restaurants, which makes the whooping crane good for the tourism industry.

COLLABORATING FOR A CAUSE

The Calgary Zoo in Canada runs a whooping crane captive breeding program at the Devonian Wildlife Conservation Centre on a ranch outside of the city. This is the only facility in Canada for whooping crane breeding. The center uses adult whooping cranes to **brood**, hatch, and raise young birds. They have seven breeding pairs that lay and incubate eggs. The zoo works closely with the other partners in the Whooping Crane Recovery Plan. In 2017, the Calgary Zoo sent nine eggs to the Patuxent Wildlife Research Center to hatch, and three birds raised in Calgary were released into the nonmigrating flock in Louisiana in 2017.

WHOOPING CRANE RANGE, 2018

WOOD BUFFALO NATIONAL PARK

CANADA

UNITED STATES

WISCONSIN

FLORIDA

ARANSAS NATIONAL WILDLIFE REFUGE

The remaining wild flock of whooping cranes breeds in Wood Buffalo National Park in Alberta, Canada, and migrates to spend the winter at Aransas on the coast of Texas. A smaller captive-bred flock breeds in Wisconsin and winters in Florida. Small, nonmigratory flocks have also been reintroduced in Louisiana and Florida.

Key

■ Breeding range

■ Wintering range

■ Reintroduced nonmigratory flock

0   620 miles
|——————|
        1,000 km

What Does the Future Hold?

In last 60 years, the whooping crane's conservation status has risen from near extinction to endangered. This success is thanks to the efforts of scientists, conservation organizations, and bird lovers. In 2016, the Calgary Zoo, the San Antonio Zoo, the International Crane Foundation, and the Audubon Nature Institute jointly won the American Zoo Association's North American Conservation Award for their work to save the whooping crane. While the whooping crane population is growing, it remains small and sensitive. If the population continues to grow, the bird's status could soon be raised to vulnerable.

The wild whooping crane population eventually needs to be able to increase on its own. The reintroduced flocks must be able to sustain themselves by breeding in the wild and raising birds that will also breed.

END OF GUIDED MIGRATION

Captive breeding and reintroduction does not work as well for whooping cranes as it has for other species. After 15 years, there were about 100 birds in the Wisconsin-Florida flock. However, a large majority of the birds introduced by Operation Migration did not survive. The International Recovery Team realized that one problem might be too much human interaction. The birds never really learn how to survive in the wild. So, in 2016, the U.S. Fish and Wildlife Service ended the aircraft-guided reintroduction program run by Operation Migration. The International Crane Foundation (headquarters, right) supported this decision.

WHOOPING CRANE POPULATION 1940-2015

Numbers of whooping cranes remained low until 1967, when the species was added to the Endangered List. Then the population began to rise more rapidly. Despite this success, the campaign still needs support. The 2018 federal budget cut funding to the United States Geological Survey (USGS).

The USGS had to cut more than $10 million from its wildlife programs. As part of these budget cuts, the Whooping Crane Propagation Program at the Patuxent Wildlife Research Center was closed down. The captive flock at Patuxent was moved to the Calgary Zoo in Alberta, Canada.

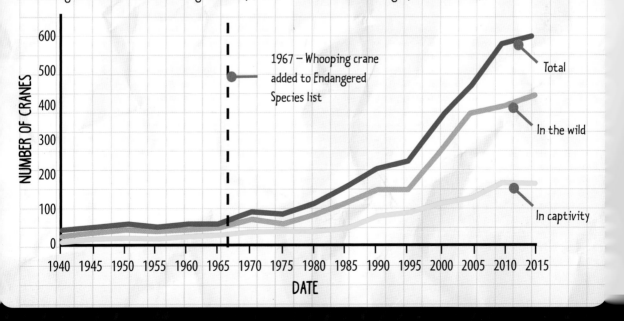

1967 – Whooping crane added to Endangered Species list

Total

In the wild

In captivity

NUMBER OF CRANES

DATE

Saving Other Species

Lessons from the story of the whooping crane can be used to help other species. Like the crane, many endangered species are bred in captivity to increase the population. One success story involving an American bird is the California condor. In 1983, when the captive breeding program began, there were only 22 condors left in the wild. Scientists took eggs from their nests to hatch and raise the birds, but the wild population continued to decline. In 1987, the last six birds in the wild were taken into captivity for their own protection, so the wild population was extinct.

The first 85 condors from the captive breeding program were released into the wild in 2003. The wild population thrived, and more captive-bred birds were released. By 2012, there were 213 California condors living in the wild and another 173 birds in captivity.

A flock of sand
is kept in capti
case a hurricane
the nesting gro
of the wild crane
conservation eff
such a disaster w
still threaten the
of the species.

LEARNING FROM EXPERIENCE

For many years, the sandhill crane was in danger of becoming extinct in North America. The International Crane Foundation helped save the sandhill by focusing on habitat protection and setting up a program for captive breeding and reintroduction. Today, the North American sandhill population is one of the largest crane populations in the world. There are successful breeding pairs throughout the bird's natural range of Mississippi, Louisiana, and Florida. Conservation scientists are figuring out how to use what they have learned about the sandhill crane to continue efforts to save the whooping crane.

Whooping Cranes Need You!

The whooping crane is back from the brink of extinction, but it is far from safe. Even the smallest threats can harm the population. Saving it will take a commitment from everyone to learn more about endangered species and habitat conservation. The more we know, the more we can help. For example, we can fight climate change and pollution by making good choices. Climate change is made worse by releasing **carbon dioxide** (CO_2) into the atmosphere. Conserving energy helps reduce CO_2 emissions.

Single-use plastic such as straws, bags, and packaging creates a lot of trash that endangers bird life all over the planet. Not only does plastic pollute their habitat, but eating it also can accidentally kill birds. Using less plastic helps to protect the environment for all endangered species.

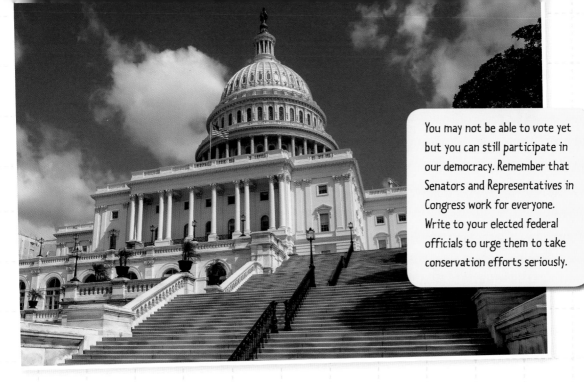

You may not be able to vote yet but you can still participate in our democracy. Remember that Senators and Representatives in Congress work for everyone. Write to your elected federal officials to urge them to take conservation efforts seriously.

SPREAD THE WORD

You might not live or travel in areas where whooping cranes live, so what can you do? Spreading information and educating people is a great way to help. Here are some ideas you can try:

- Use the websites of conservation organizations such as the International Crane Foundation to get updates about their work. You can follow these organizations on social media and share their posts with your friends. Look for the hashtags #GiveAWhoop and #SavetheCrane on Facebook, Twitter, and Instagram.

- Contact your local elected officials to tell them that wildlife and habitat protection are important to your future. Elected representatives can help by opposing funding cuts to conservation programs and agencies such as the Environmental Protection Agency in the United States. Elected representatives can also vote to protect legislation such as the Clean Water Act and Endangered Species Act in the United States and Canada's Environmental Protection Act.

- If you live near the breeding grounds and flyways of the whooping crane, ask your local government about efforts to protect the wetlands that migrating whooping cranes need to survive.

Learning More

Books

Goodman, Susan A. *Saving the Whooping Crane. On My Own Science.* National Geographic School Publishing, 2010.

Johnsgard, Paul A. *Sandhill and Whooping Cranes: Ancient Voices over America's Wetlands.* Bison Books, 2011.

Nigge, Klaus. *Whooping Crane: Images from the Wild.* Texas A&M University Press, 2010.

Sanders, Lynn. *Dancing with Tex—The Remarkable Friendship to Save the Whooping Cranes.* Difference Maker's Media, 2016.

On the Web

www.savingcranes.org
The website of the International Crane Foundation, which is dedicated to conserving cranes and their habitat.

whoopingcrane.com
The website of the original Whooping Crane Conservation Association, the first organization devoted to protecting the crane.

www.audubon.org
The website of the National Audubon Society, the leading U.S. bird conservation organization.

friendsofthewildwhoopers.org
Pages run by the conservation organization dedicated to protecting the Aransas–Wood Buffalo population of wild whooping cranes.

www.whoopingcranefestival.org
The website of the annual whooping crane festival held in the city of Port Aransas, Texas.

www.calgaryzoo.com
The Calgary Zoo is home to Canada's only whooping crane breeding center. This site contains details of the zoo's work with cranes and other endangered species.

For videos, activities, and more, enter the access code at the Crabtree Plus website below.

www.crabtreeplus.com/animals-back-brink

Access code: abb37

Glossary

artificial insemination A process in which a scientist uses male sperm to fertilize the eggs of a female by inserting the sperm in a laboratory

brood For a bird to sit on eggs to keep them warm before they hatch

captivity A situation in which an animal is held in a zoo or conservation center and taken care of by humans

carbon dioxide A gas produced by breathing and by burning carbon, usually in the form of fossil fuels such as gas and coal

climate change A gradual change in the global climate caused in part by human activity

conservation Preserving and using resources wisely

costume method A way of rearing captive birds in which human handlers wear bird costumes

cultivation The artificial breeding and planting of plants, such as crops

decline A fall in the number of something

drought A period in which there is little or no rainfall in an area that usually has rain

ecosystem All living things in a particular area and how they interact

extinct Describes a situation in which all members of a species have died, so the species no longer exists

flock A group of the same type of birds that live and travel together

flyway A route regularly followed by migrating birds

habitat The conditions in which an animal or plant naturally lives

imprint A process by which a young animal recognizes another animal as being its parent

migrates The movement, especially by an animal, from one place to another—usually according to seasonal changes

natural resources Materials that are found in nature and can be used by humans

ornithologist A scientist who studies bird biology and behavior

predators Animals that hunt other animals for food

range The region where an animal can be found

species A group of animals or plants that are similar to each other

ultra-light aircraft A very small, low-speed airplane that has an open frame and just one or two seats

wetlands Regions that are usually damp or flooded with water

Index and About the Author

ABOUT THE AUTHOR

Rachel Stuckey is a writer and editor with 15 years of experience in educational publishing. She has written more than 25 books for young readers on topics ranging from science to sports, and works with subject matter experts to develop educational resources in both the sciences and humanities. Rachel travels for half the year, working on projects while exploring the world and learning about our global community.